Pastel Etudes

Stevan

40 Pastel Paintings On Paper

Cover: Eye to Eye

S

Modern Man

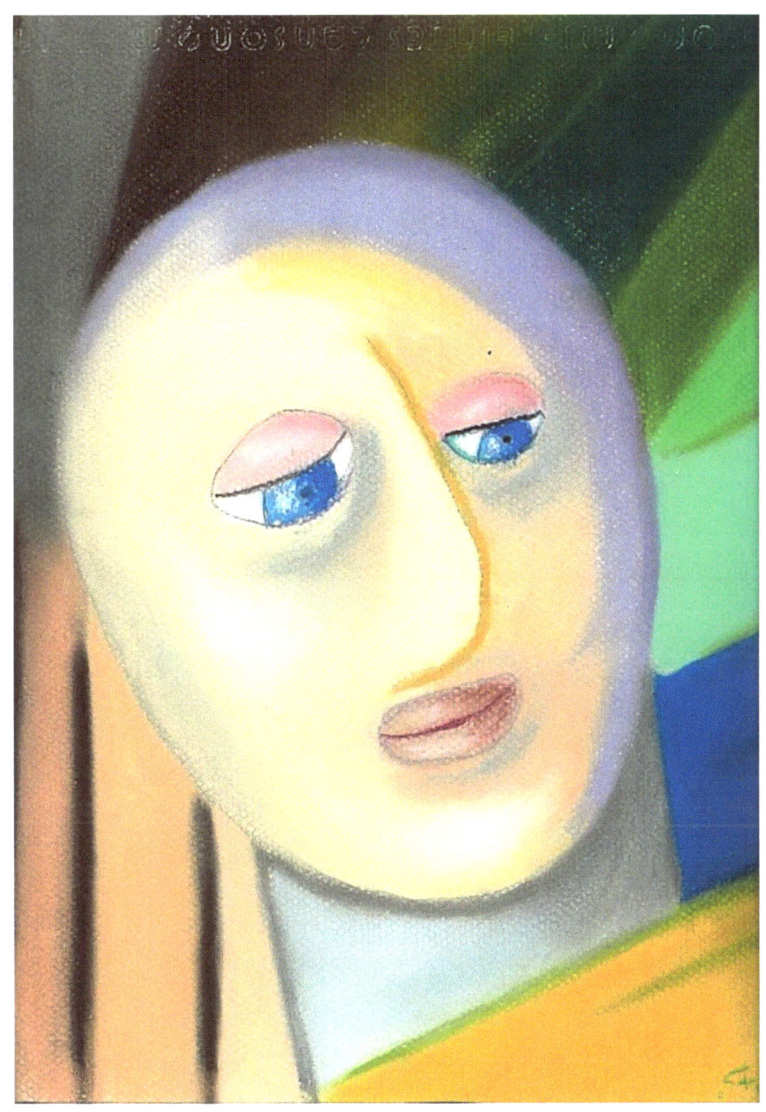

S

Moth

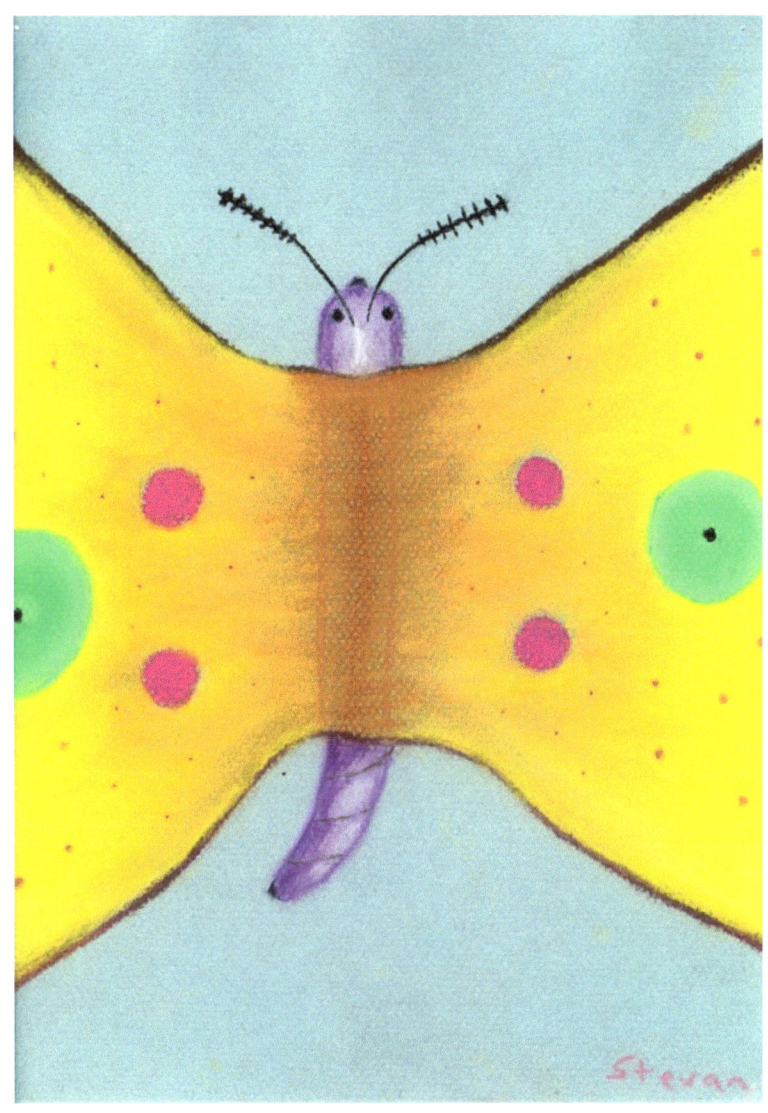

S

High Fashion

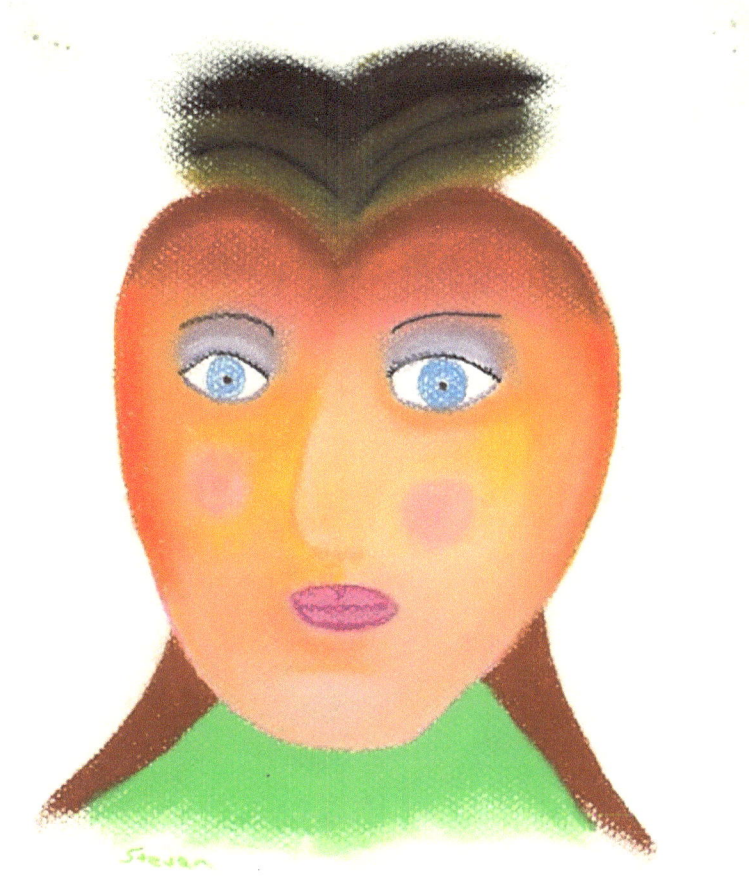

S

Eye on Earth

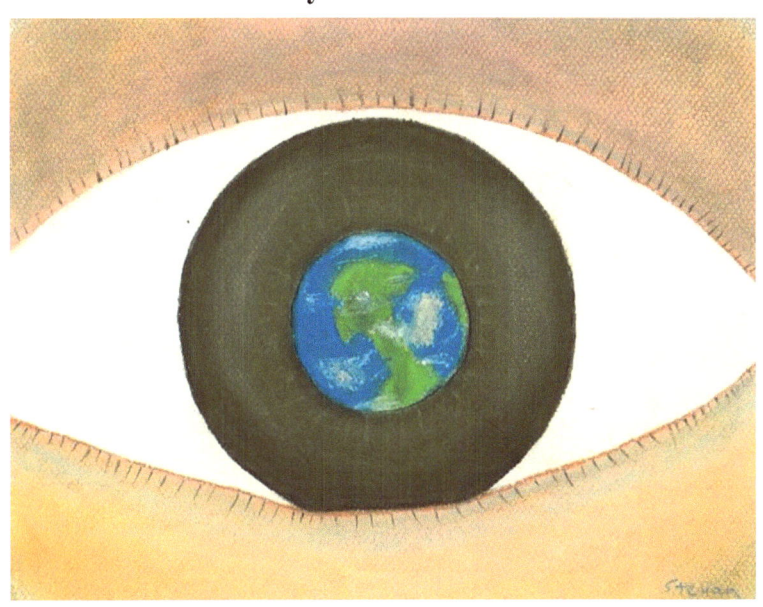

S

Java

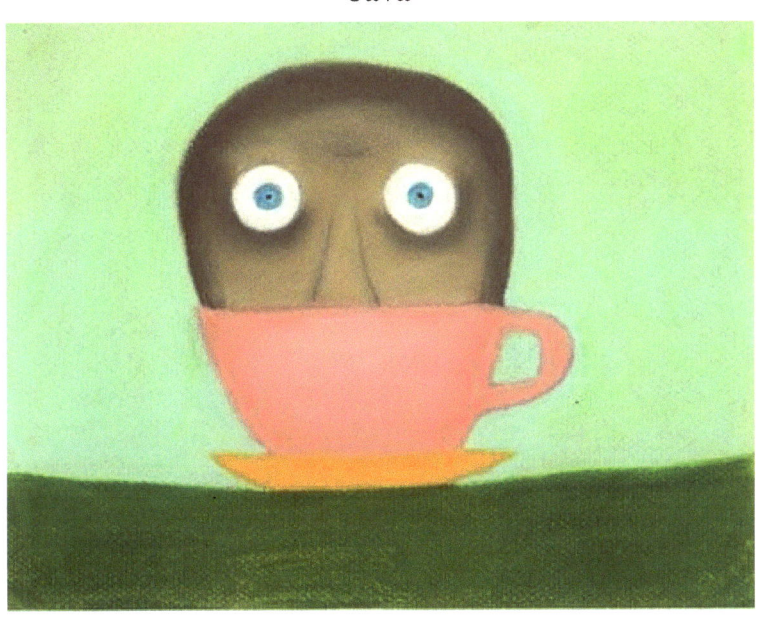

S

Wolfman

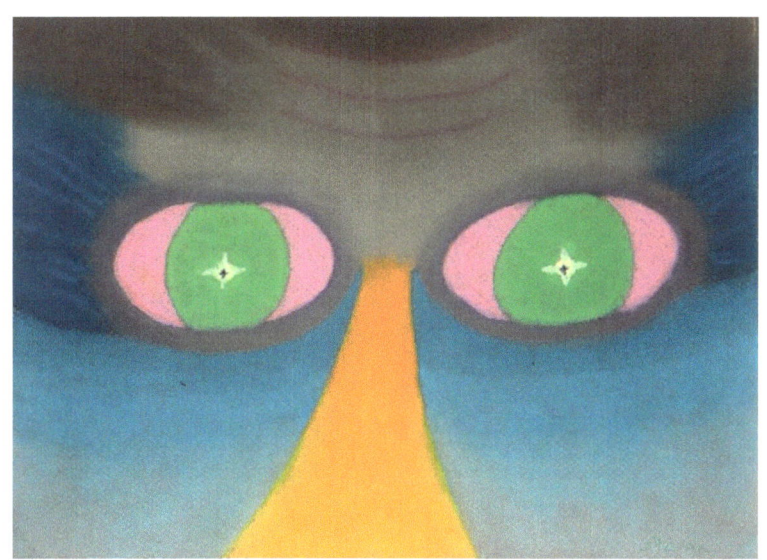

S

Nest

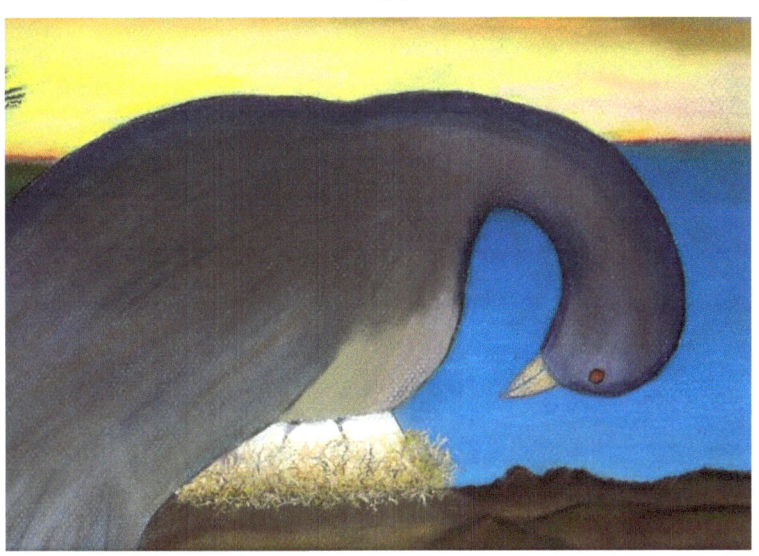

S

Flower Power

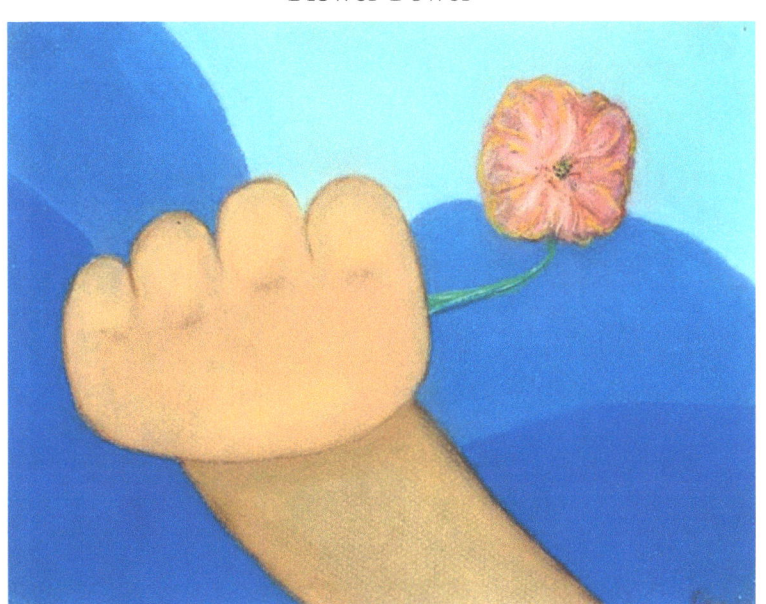

S

Rose

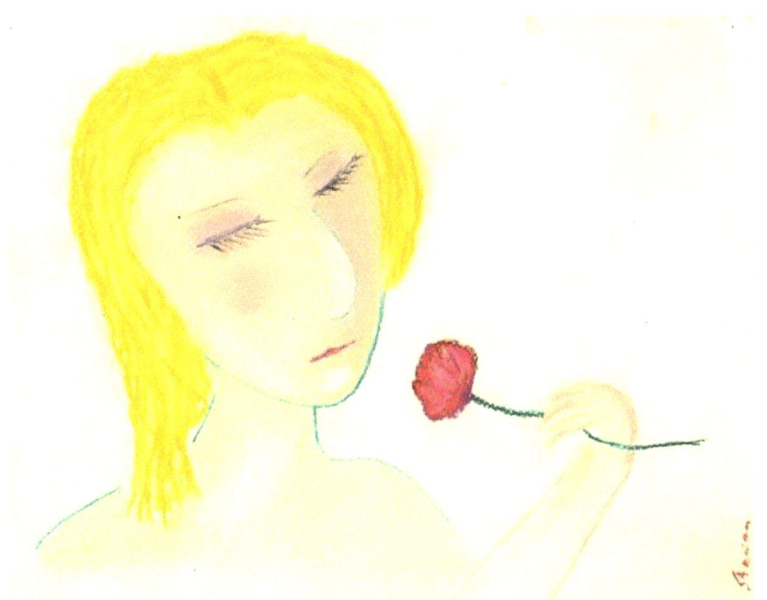

S

Bouquet

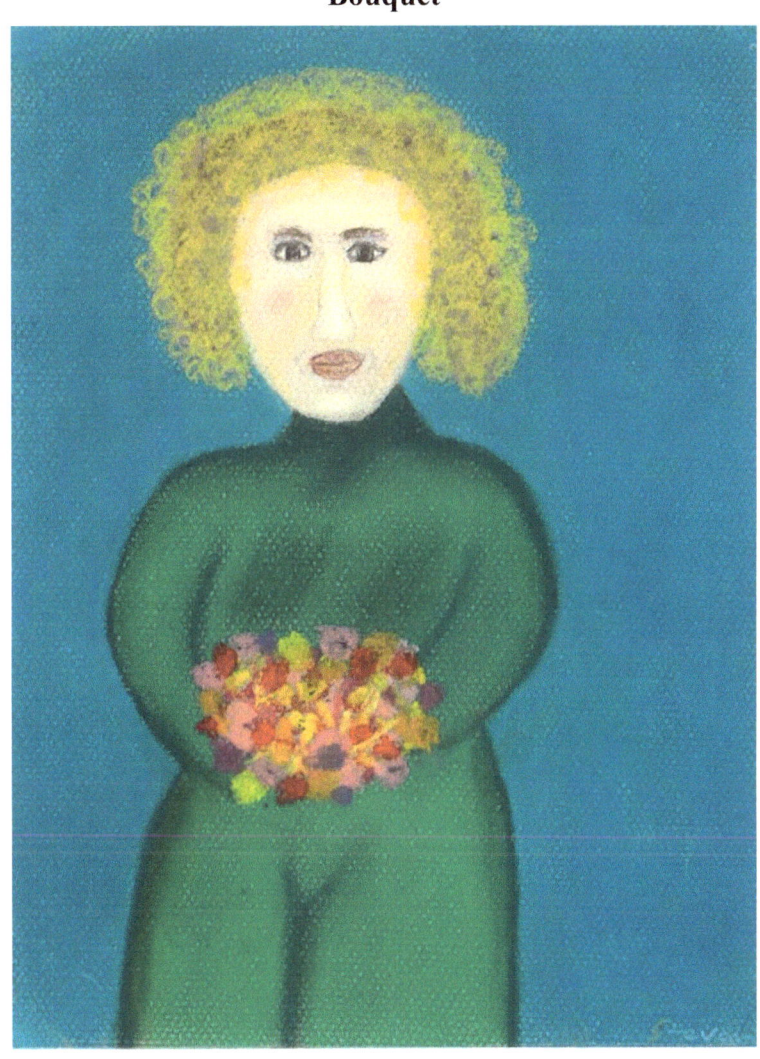

S

Depression

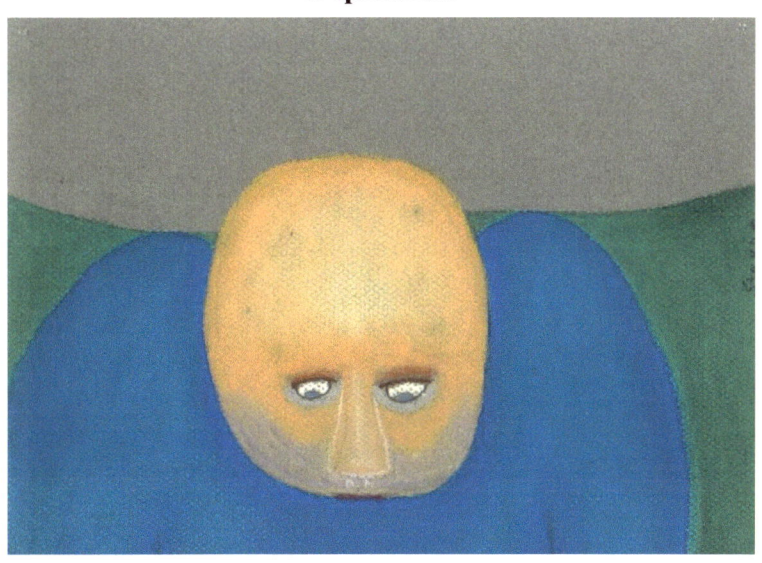

S

Bonanza

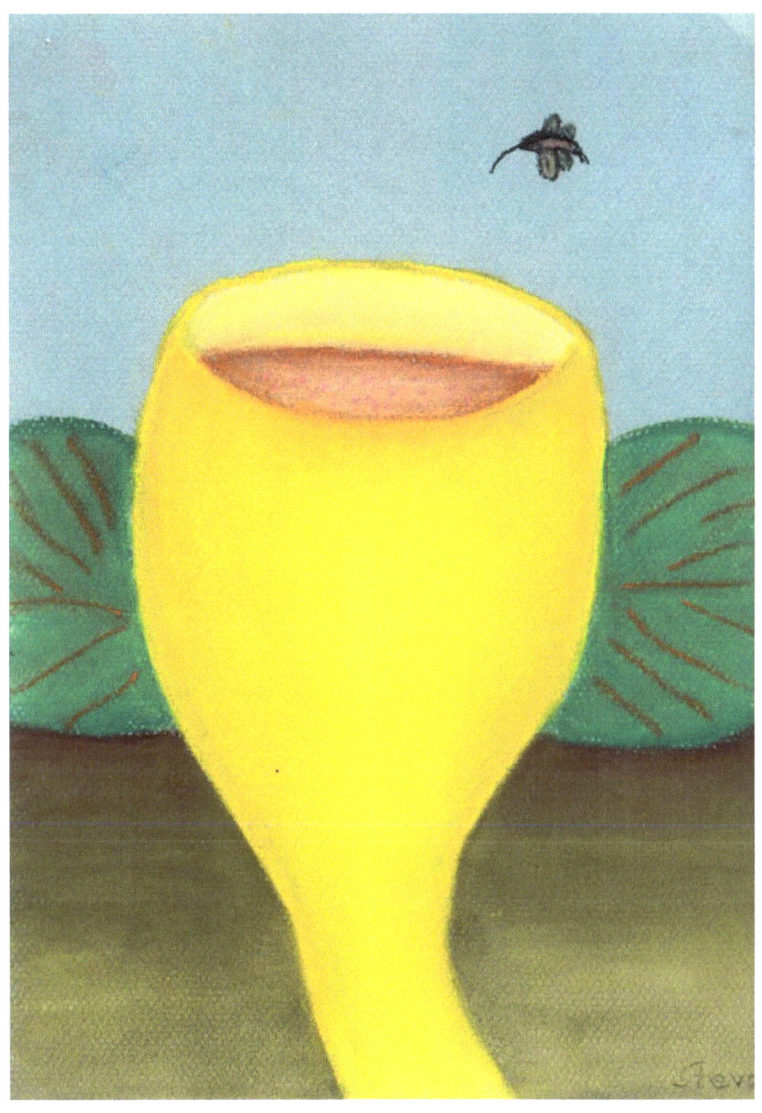

Convict

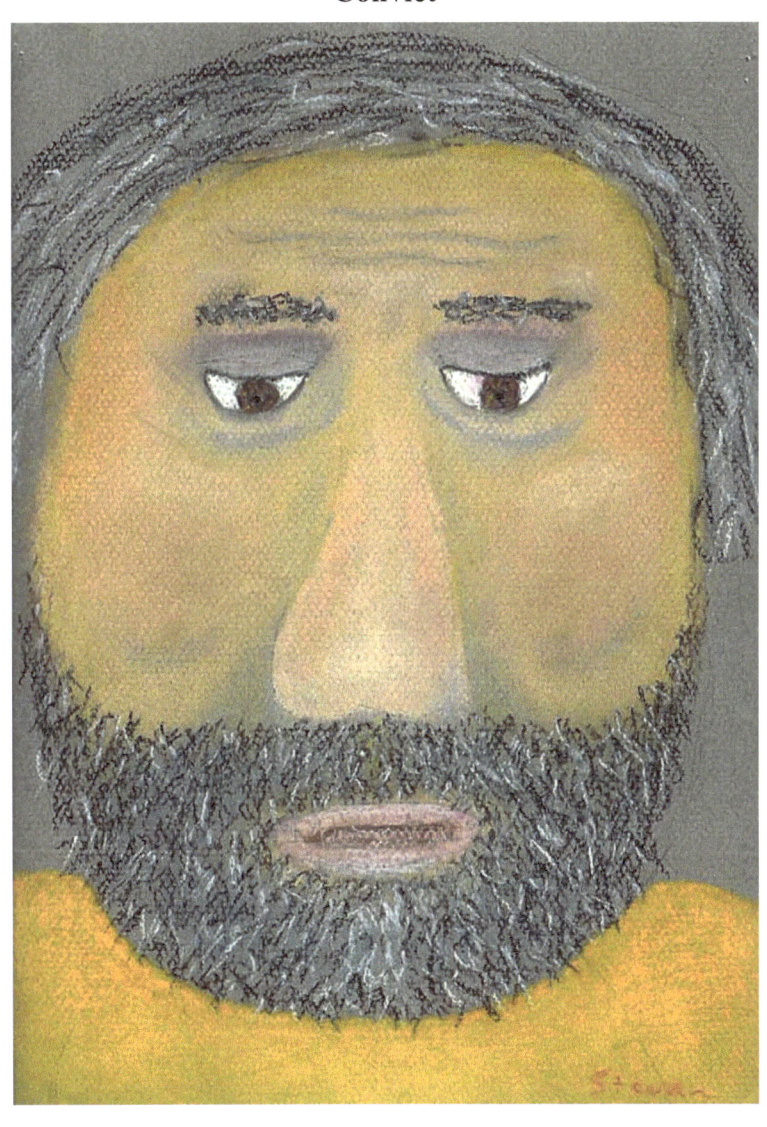

S

Purgatory

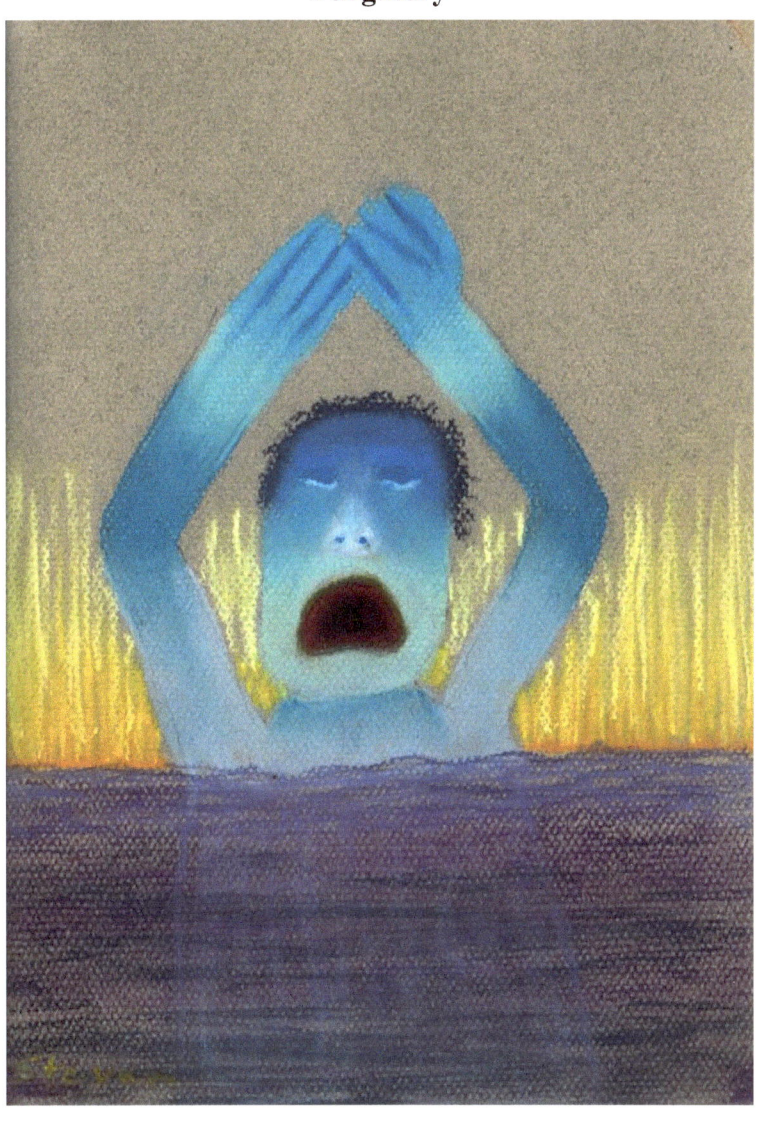

S

Leaves

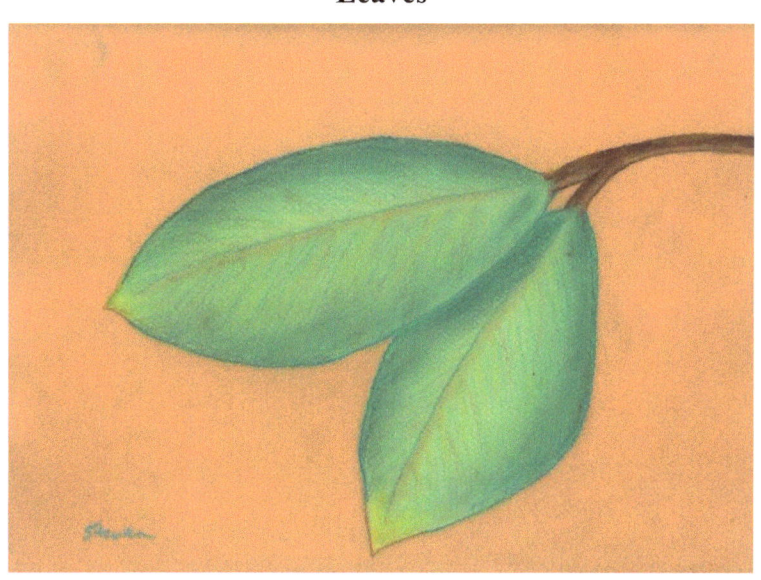

S

Vacation

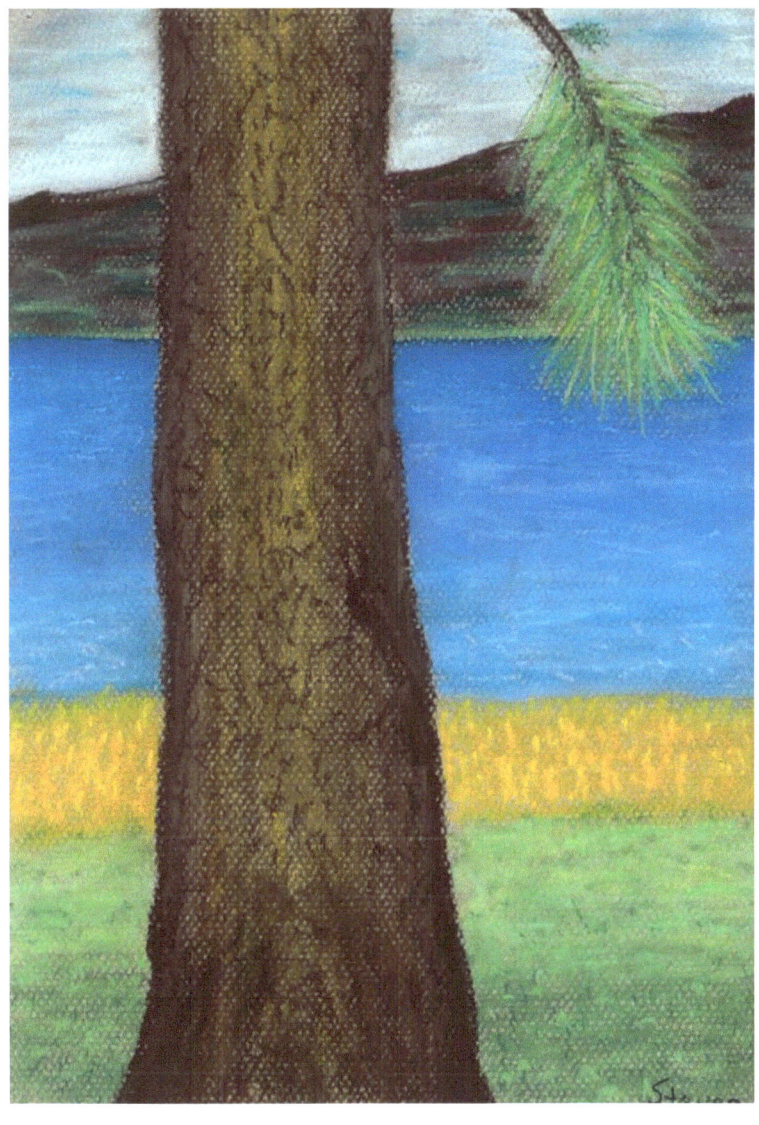

S

Civilization

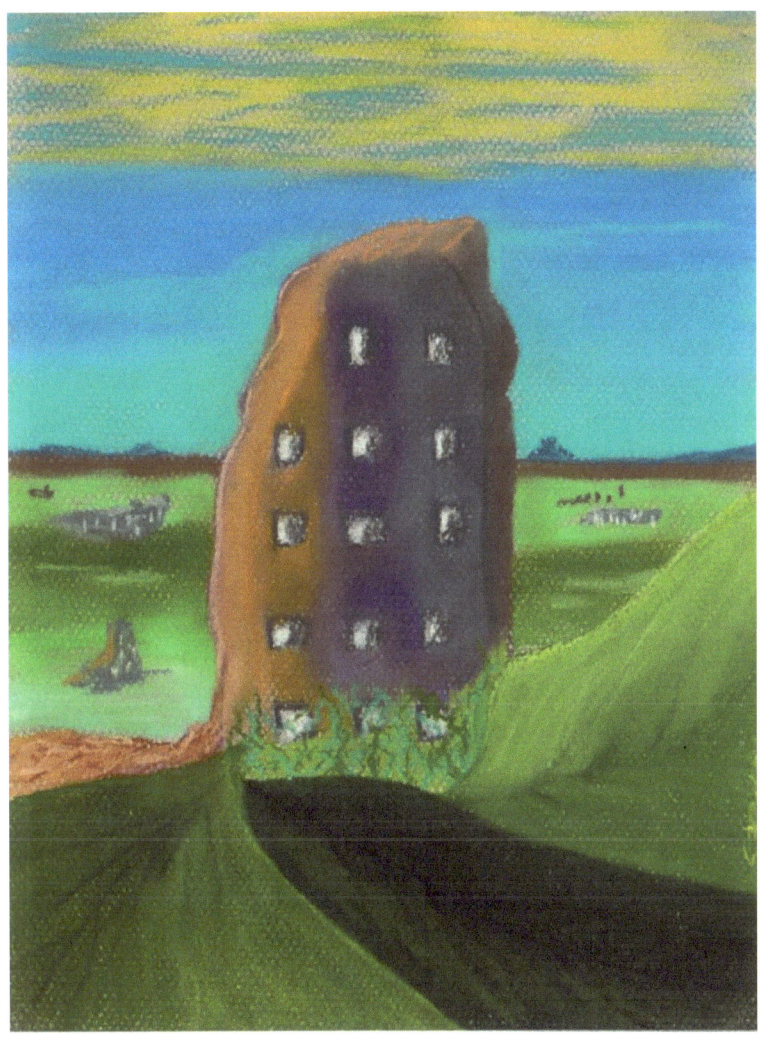

S

Hear No Evil

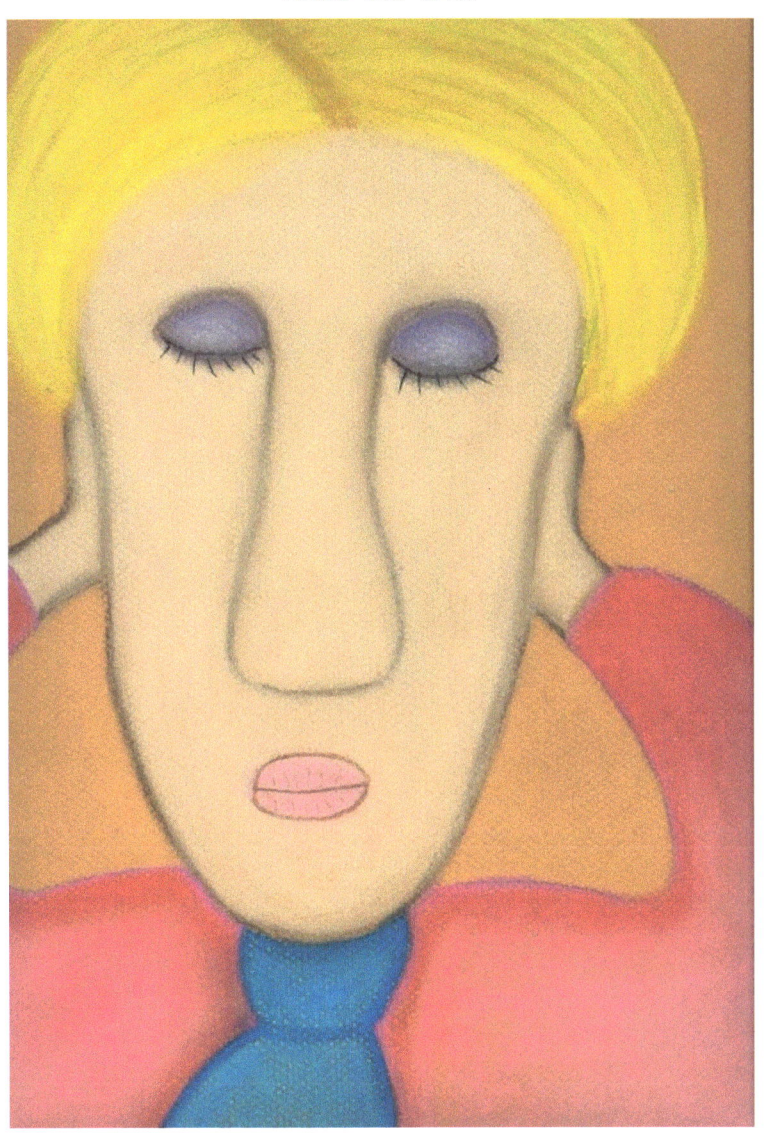

S

Bird in Hand

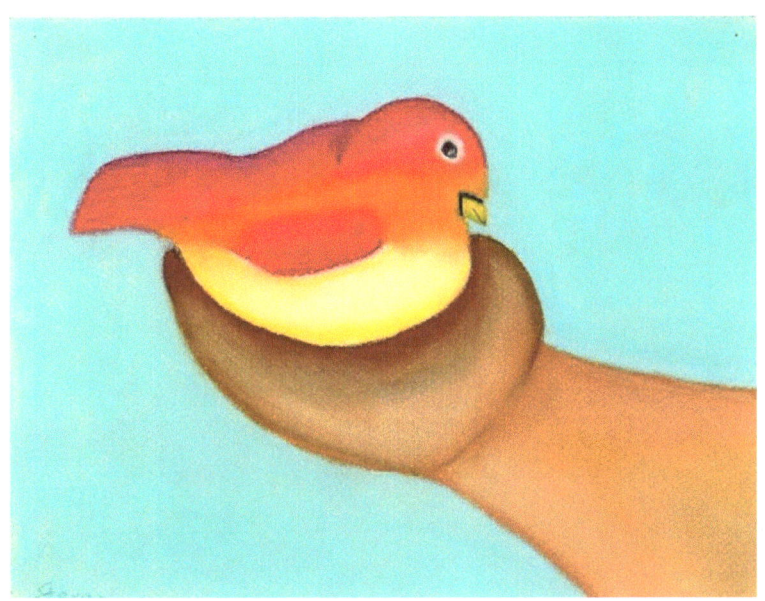

S

Highway

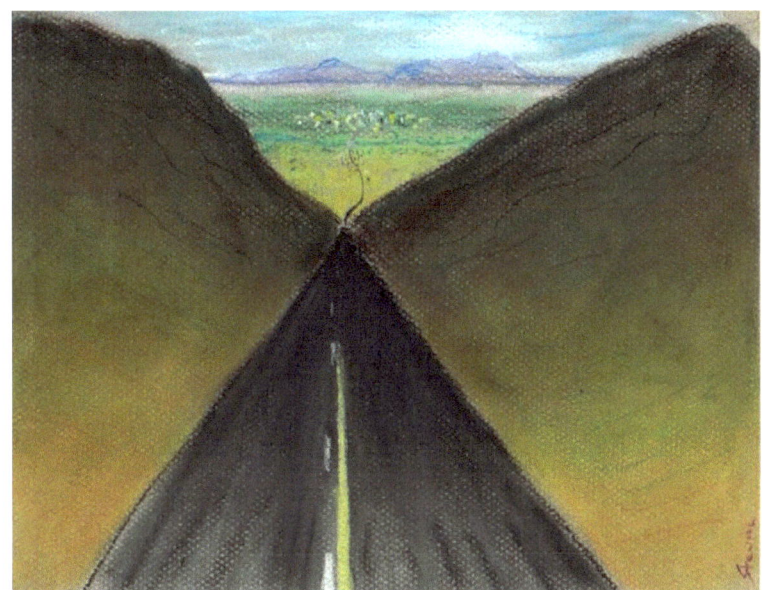

S

Nude

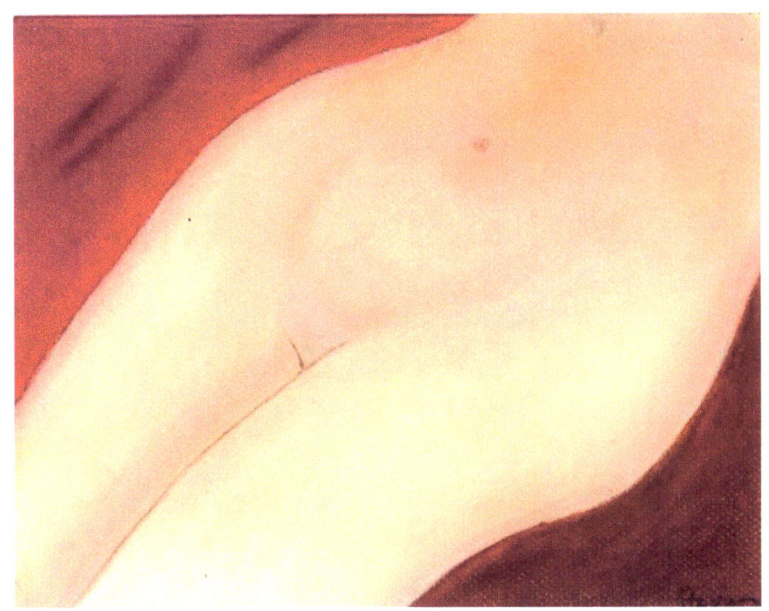

S

I'M right

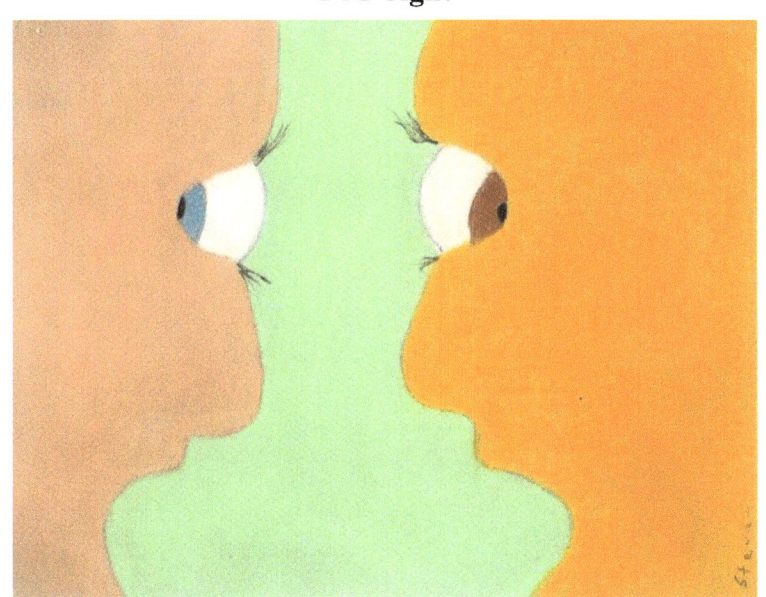

S

Cosmos

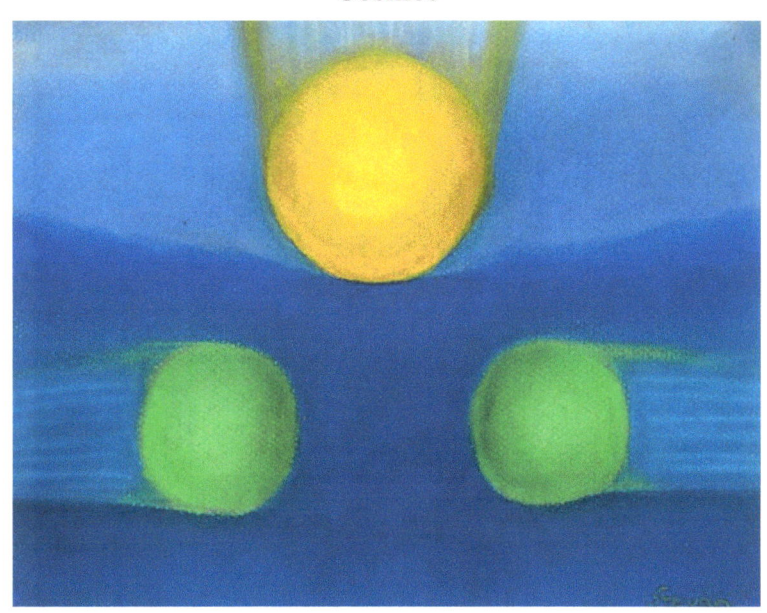

S

Tipping Point

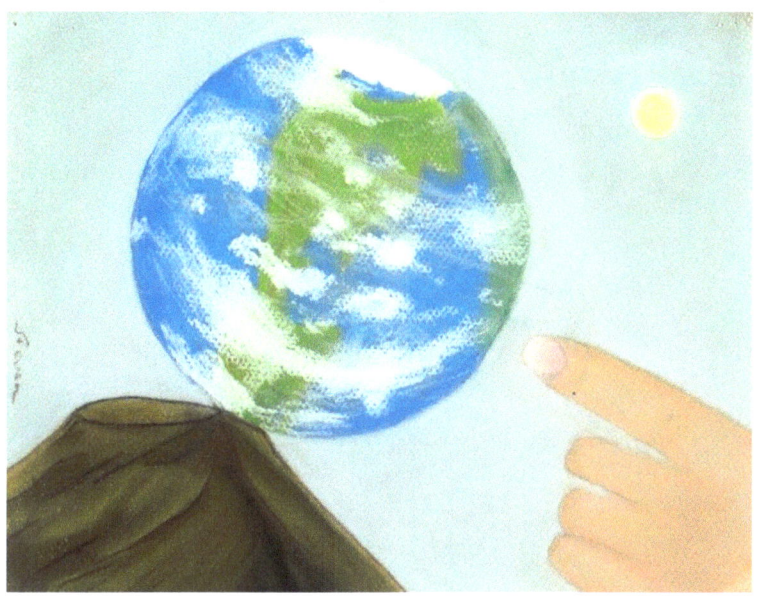

S

Nectar

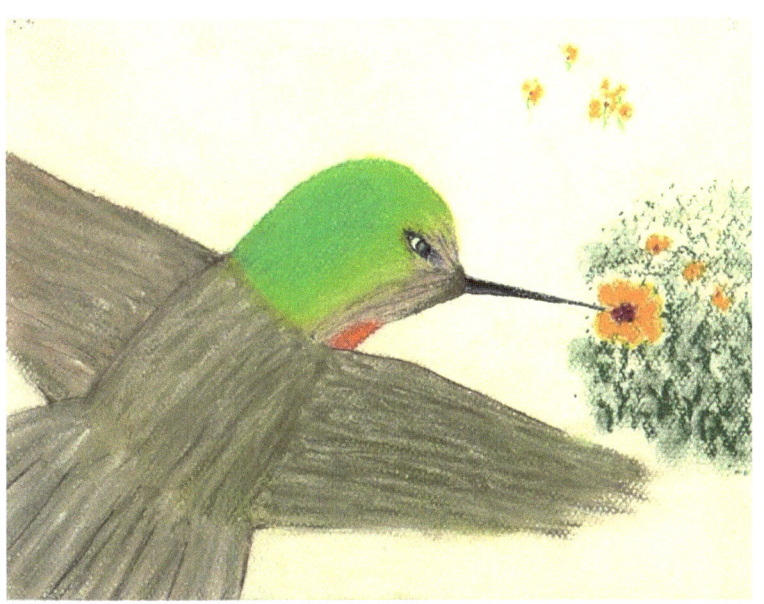

S

Prophecy

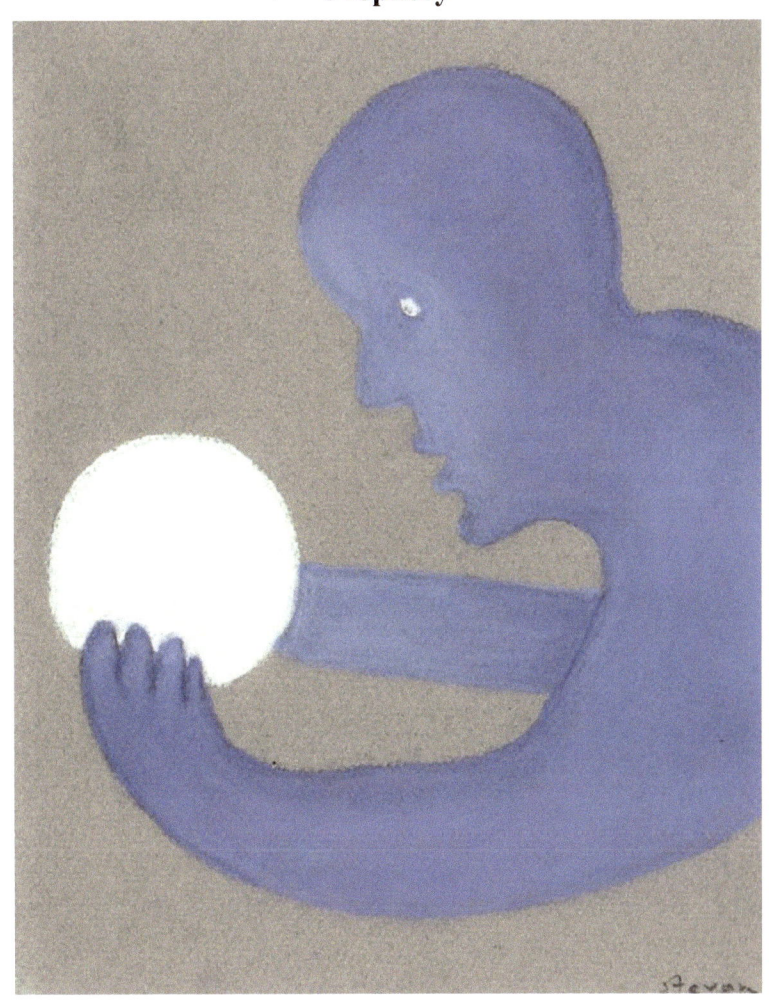

S

Election

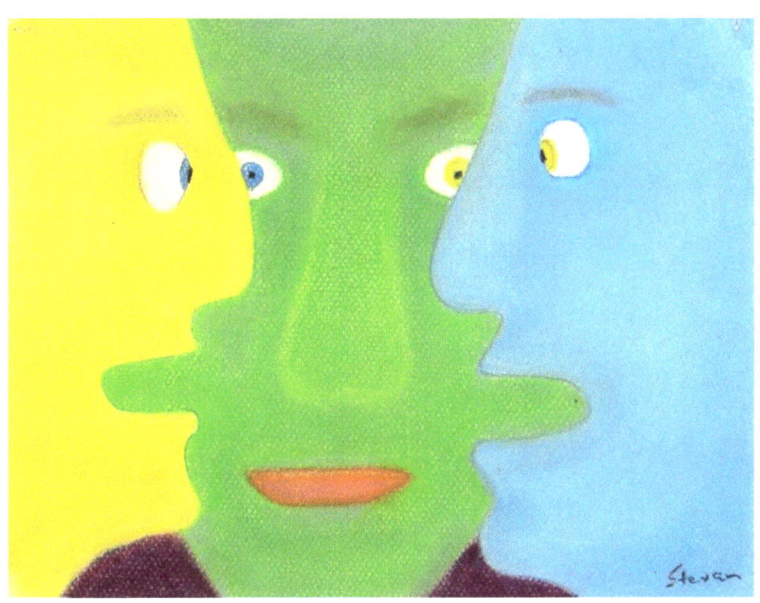

S

Shy

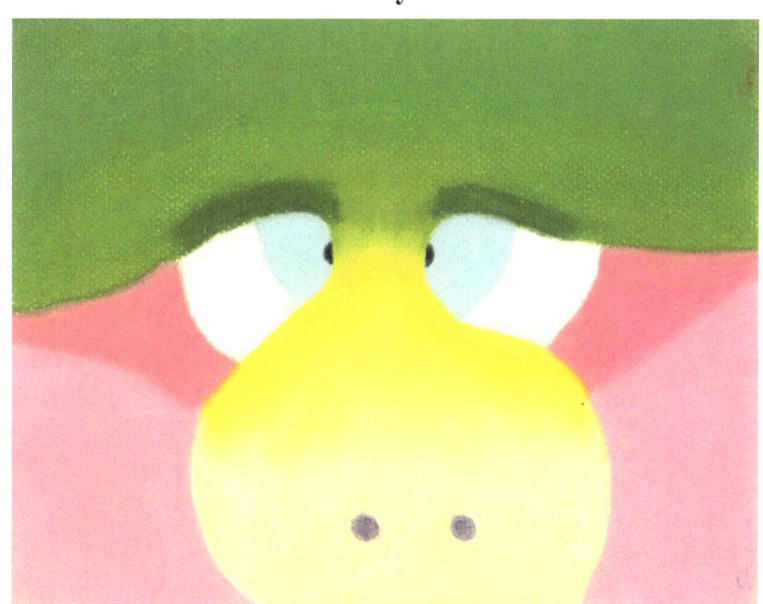

S

Petal

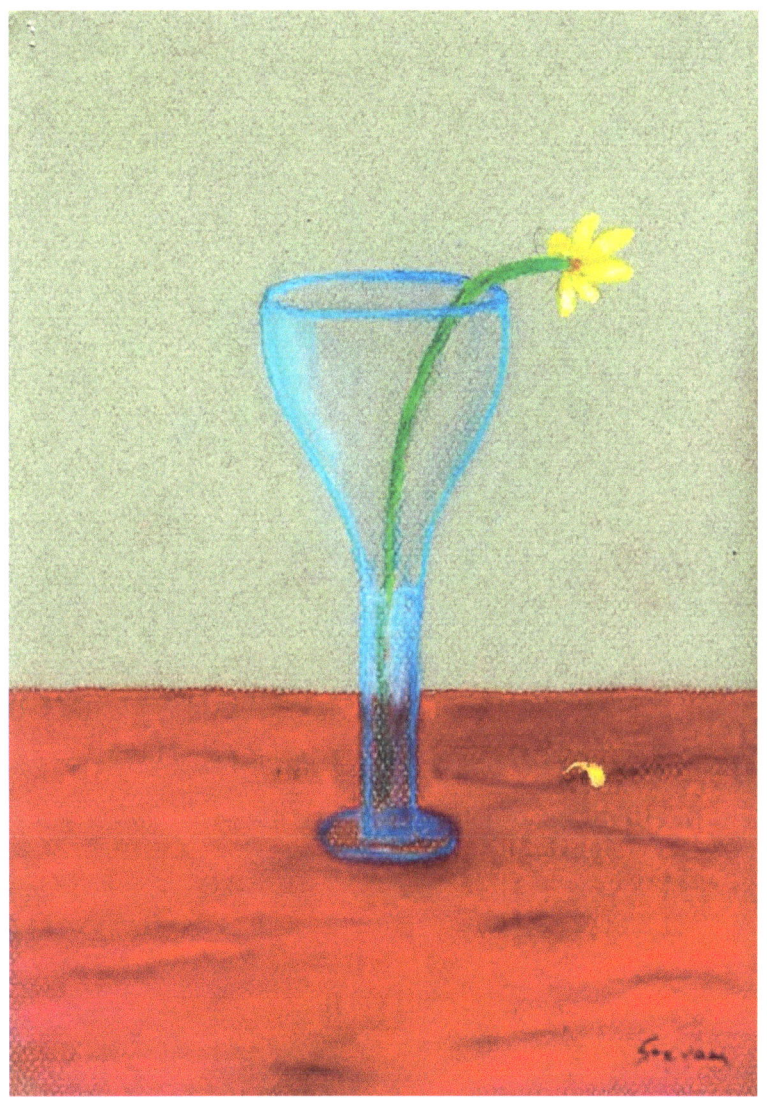

S

Yellow Hair

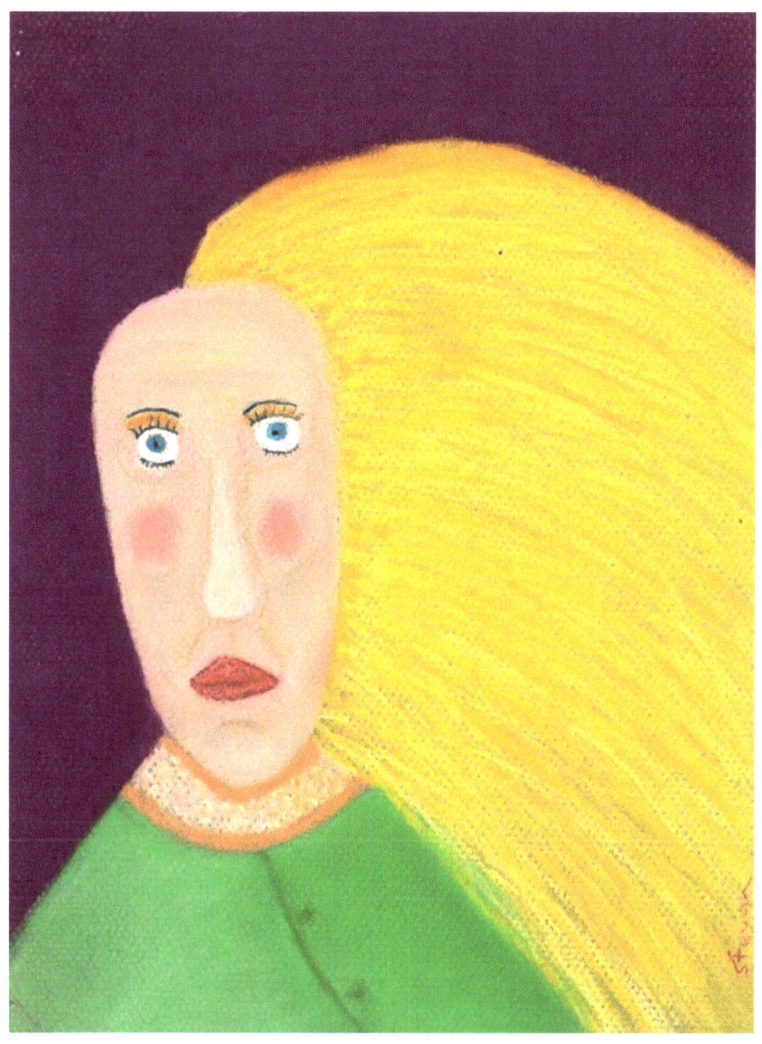

S

Condemned

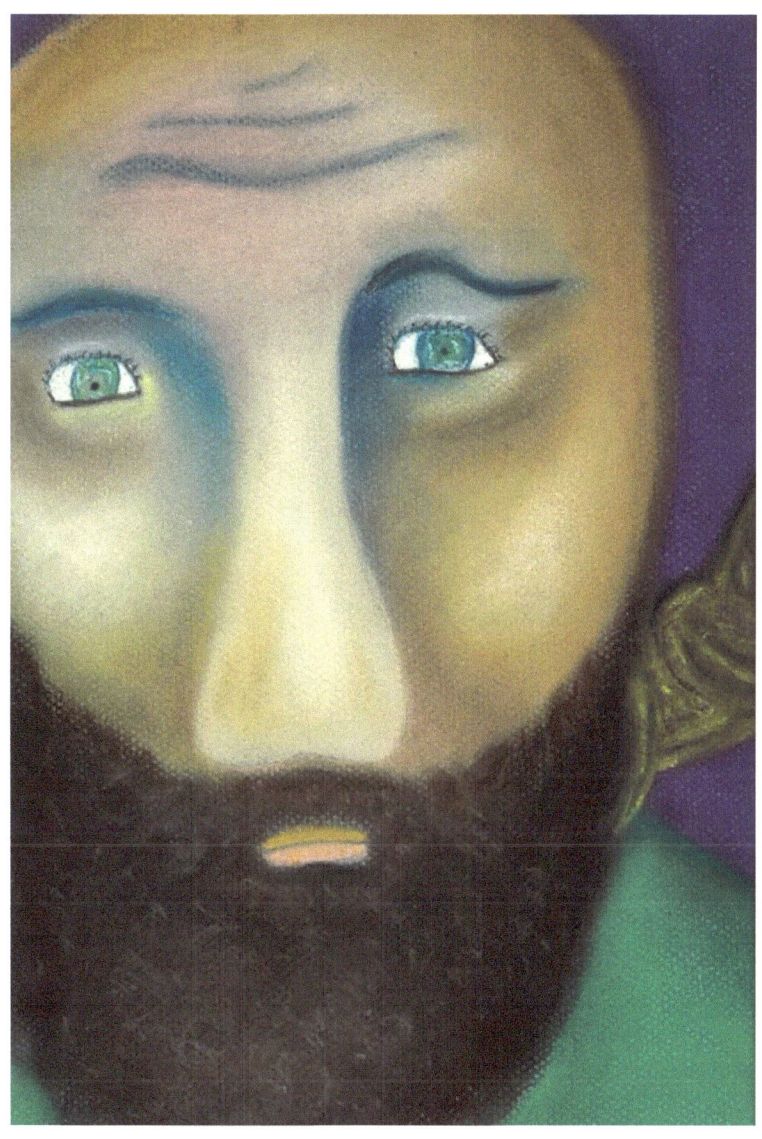

S

Half Alive

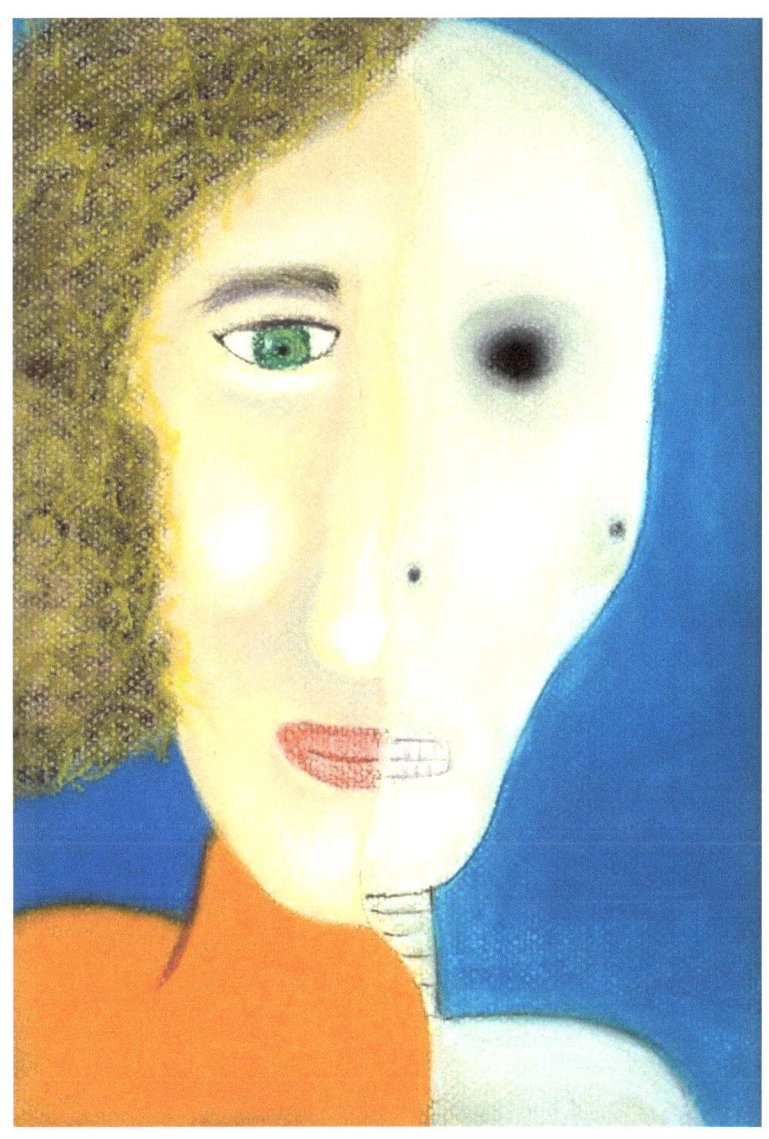

S

Tequila Sunrise

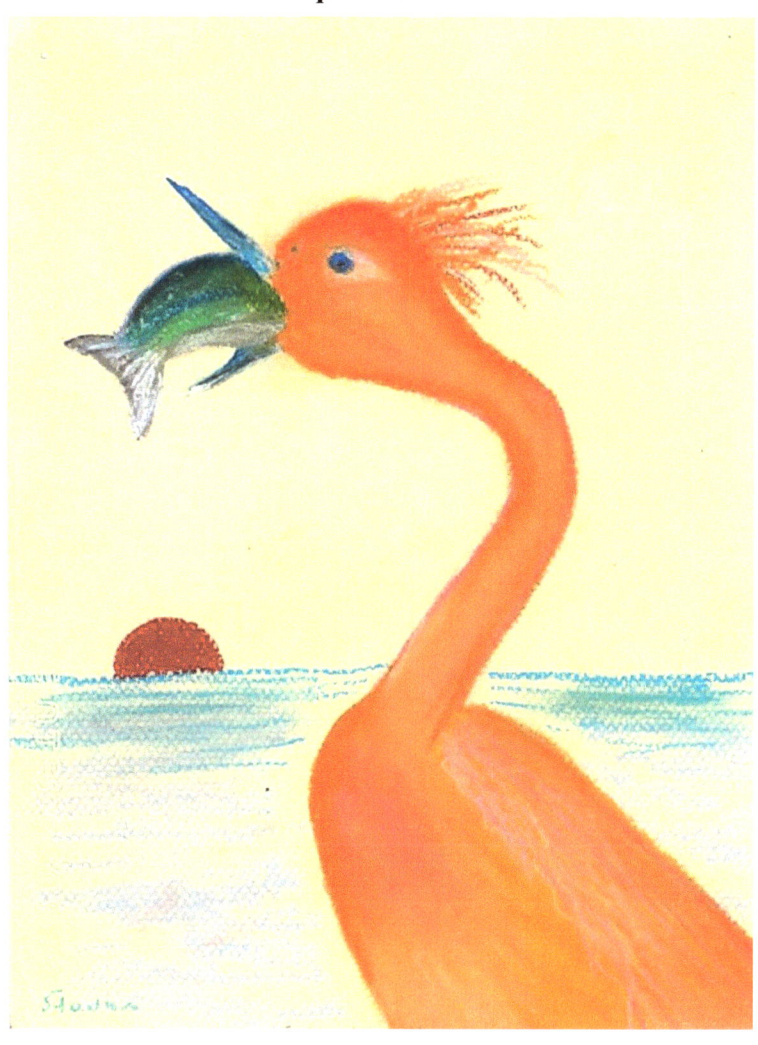

S*

Nirvana

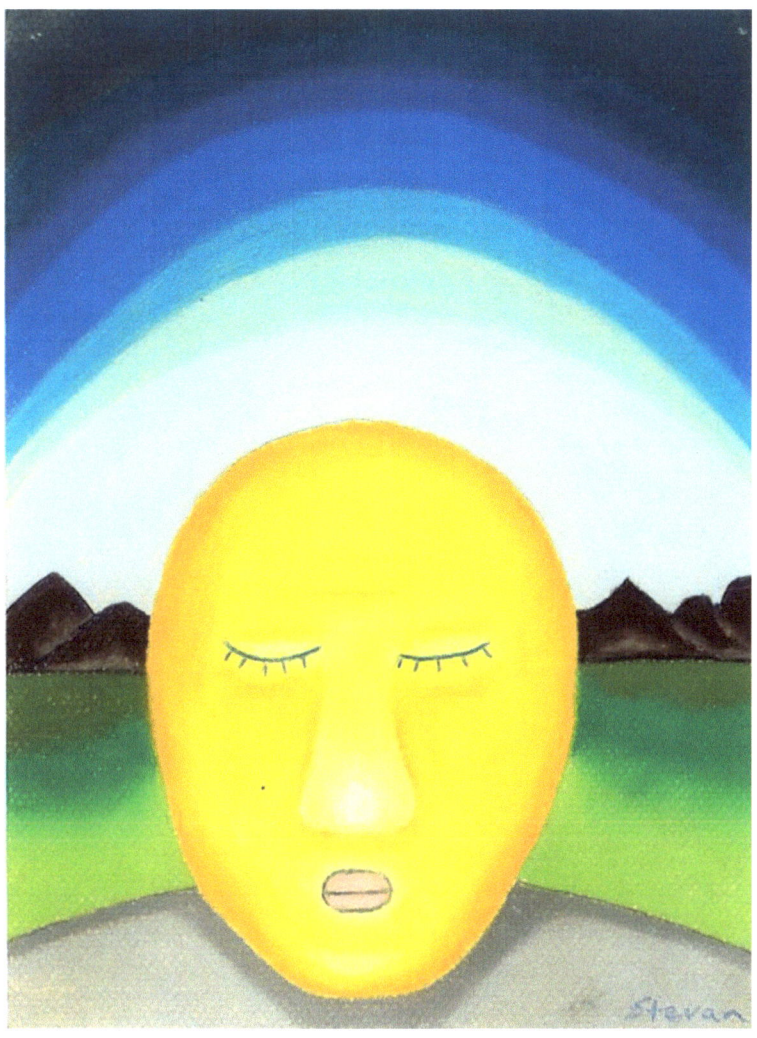

S

Genetics

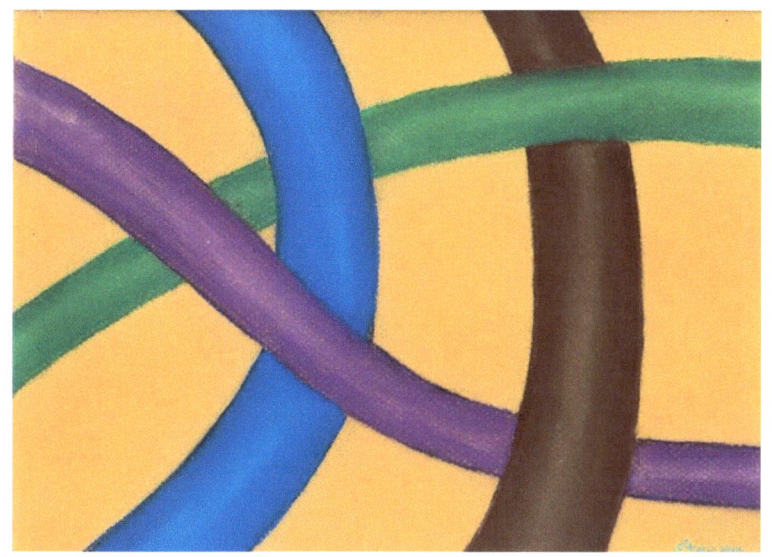

S

Grief

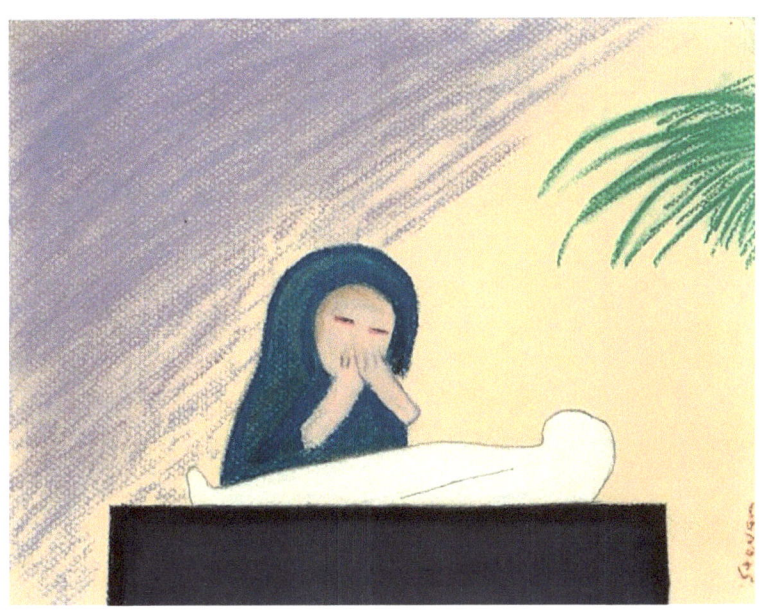

S

Hope

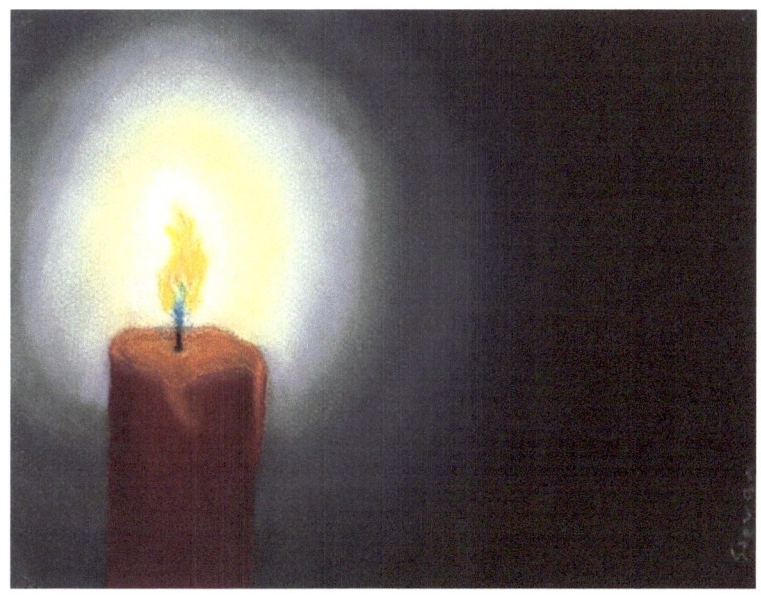

S

Lava

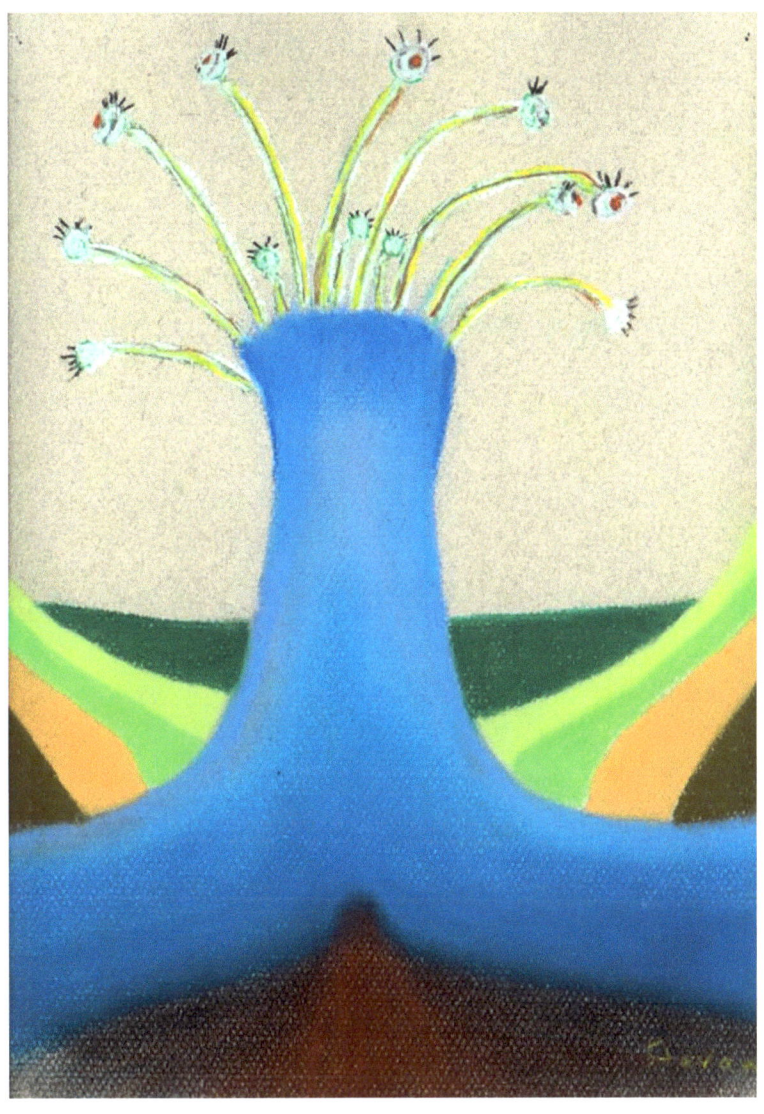

S

Fish Birth

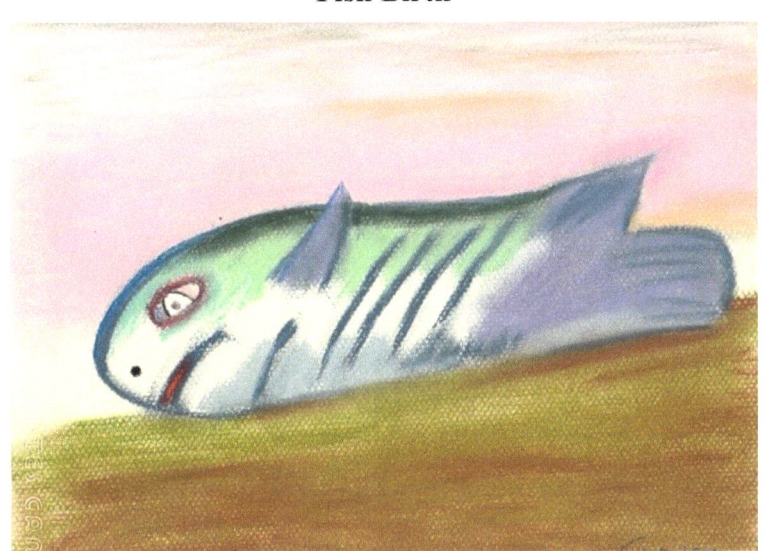